Do·It·Yourself
HOME
INSULATION

Blandford Press
Poole·Dorset

Series Editor: Mike Lawrence
Author: Jill Thomas

Editorial production by Keith Faulkner Publishing Limited

© Aura Books Limited 1985

This edition first published by
Blandford Press 1985
Link House
West Street
Poole Dorset

Printed and bound by Henri Proost, Turnhout, Belgium

Contents

The great escape

If your fuel bills seem harder to face each time they fall through the letter box, this book's for you. It shows you where and how to insulate your home as a means to lower heating bills. Many insulation jobs are easy to do and pay dividends in reduced fuel bills – year after year. Even if your home already has some degree of insulation, this book can be of use for there are few houses which couldn't benefit from more insulation somewhere.

All the heat you put into your house is eventually lost to the outside. It happens as warm, heated air escapes and is replaced by fresh, cold air and as surfaces warmed on the inside are cooled by cold air outside. Insulating is a way of reducing the rate at which the heat is lost. You can't stop it escaping altogether, but you can slow it down to an acceptable rate.

The more slowly the warm air escapes, the less heat you have to put in and the lower your fuel bills will be during the winter minths.

Heat escapes from an uninsulated building through different parts of the structure in varying proportions. The exact proportions depend, of course, on the type of house, if you

Heat is lost in different proportions through the house walls, roof and windows, some even escapes through the ground floors

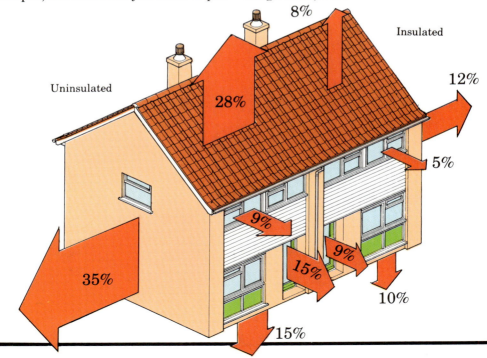

live in a terraced house less will go through the walls than if you live in a detached house; in a bungalow, more will go through the loft than in a two-storey house. The drawing on the facing page shows the average amount of heat lost through each part of the house. The drawing below shows how the heat loss can be reduced by the insulation measures described in this book.

In a fully insulated house the amount of heat lost is considerably reduced

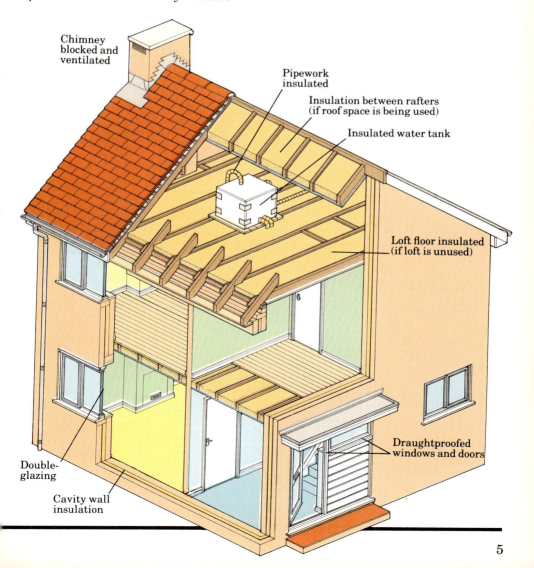

Chimney blocked and ventilated

Pipework insulated

Insulation between rafters (if roof space is being used)

Insulated water tank

Loft floor insulated (if loft is unused)

Draughtproofed windows and doors

Double-glazing

Cavity wall insulation

You might think that the places to start insulating are those which lose the most heat, but this isn't so. In deciding which insulating jobs to do first, you need to take into account what each is going to cost. The jobs which save enough on your fuel bills to pay for themselves in the shortest time are the ones to do first.

In the chart facing, there's an idea of the time it takes to recoup the cost of stopping each escape route. And in the following pages these insulating jobs are covered in priority order.

The main reason for insulating is, of course, to save money on bills for heating fuel, but there are other

A well insulated home not only saves on heating bills, but is much more comfortable to live in.

benefits too.

Insulating walls and windows increases the temperature of their indoor surfaces. Higher surface temperatures mean you'll be comfortably warm with lower air temperatures – so you can turn down the heating. You should also find that it is more comfortable to sit near to windows and walls that have been insulated. Cutting out draughts around doors and windows also increases the amount of a room that you can com-

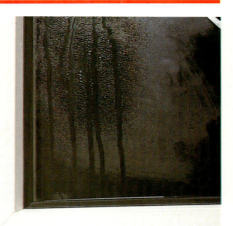

When warm moist air meets a cold surface condensation is the result.

fortably use in your home.

If parts of your house suffer from condensation, higher surface temperatures should help to reduce it. But this isn't always so; in some cases insulation can actually increase the amount of condensation – see page 22.

Where heat escapes

	heat lost	**time to recoup cost**
cracks and gaps	about a sixth	around a year
roofs	about a quarter	about 2 years
floors	about a sixth	2 or 3 years
walls	about a third	2 to 5 years
windows	about a tenth	around 8 years for most d-i-y types

Hot water cylinder

Before you turn your attention to insulating the rest of the house, check out your hot water cylinder. About a fifth of your fuel bill goes on heating water for washing and if the cylinder is uninsulated or inadequately insulated, it could be costing you a fortune in wasted heat.

You need insulation around your hot water cylinder to a minimum thickness of 80mm.

You can buy hot water cylinders with moulded-on insulation, but unless yours has been installed fairly recently, it is probably the bare-metal type. It can be insulated by fitting a purpose-made jacket or by building a box to be filled with a loose-fill material such as vermiculite.

The more layers of insulation you have around your cylinder the better. So, if your cylinder already has some insulation – a jacket 50mm thick perhaps – fit the new insulation over it. Once you've insulated, use any space around and over the cylinder as a home for spare bedding. This will help to keep the bedding aired as well as insulating the cylinder. Don't pack the bedding in too tightly, a loose fit will give better insulation.

FITTING A JACKET

Choose a jacket that conforms to British Standard 5615:1978 – the British Standard Kitemark is a sign of this. Get the right size jacket for your cylinder. Most are either 36in by 18in or 42in by 18in – the larger dimension is the height measured from the bottom of the cylinder to the start of its dome.

Jackets are generally made in padded segments joined by a tie collar at the top and held in place by one or two belts round the body of the cylinder. Fitting one is very simple, but make sure that the segments cover the whole cylinder, the parts at the back which you can't see as well as the front. Fit the jacket so that the segments butt or overlap slightly with no gaps between. Take care not to squash the insulation or fasten it too tightly. If there is an immersion heater, keep the jacket clear of the heater's cap and the electric cable.

Fitting a hot water cylinder jacket is a quick and easy way to save on heating bills, and keep the water hot longer.

LOOSE-FILL INSULATION

If you would have difficulty fitting a jacket, construct a box around the cylinder using hardboard and timber battens. Fill the box with vermiculite insulation, remembering to keep the insulation clear of the immersion heater cap and its cable. It may be possible to use the walls of the cupboard containing the cylinder as one or more sides of the box.

Cut hardboard panels to form the sides of the box. Make a frame of timber battens screwed together at the corners and pin the hardboard to the frame.

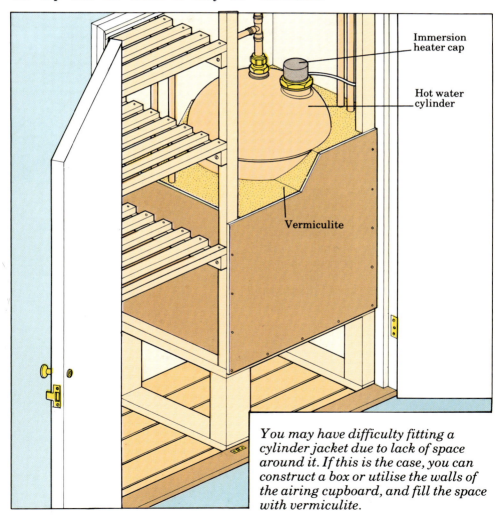

Immersion heater cap

Hot water cylinder

Vermiculite

You may have difficulty fitting a cylinder jacket due to lack of space around it. If this is the case, you can construct a box or utilise the walls of the airing cupboard, and fill the space with vermiculite.

Cracks and gaps

The cracks and gaps about your house are a source of whistling draughts. And, although individually they don't seem much, in the average house they can add up to the equivalent of a hole about a third of the size of your front door. Put like that, it becomes clear why draught excluding is just about the best insulation measure you can take. The job is simple to do, the materials aren't expensive and you should recover their cost in lower fuel bills in about a year.

There are all sorts of gaps around a house through which you will be losing heat. External doors and windows are obvious and these should be your priorities, but don't forget

- loft hatches

- gaps around pipes passing through the ceiling into the loft

- internal doors – not all your internal doors will need doing, the ones to think about are: doors to rooms you heat to higher temperatures than the rest of the house – your main living room perhaps; doors to unheated parts of the house – rooms you don't normally heat, the understairs cupboard, any eaves cupboards or a larder

- letterboxes

- cat flaps

- fireplaces

Cracks and gaps in floors can also cause draughts – see page 46.

If you want to prove to yourself that there are draughts coming in, or to check that your draughtproofing has been effective, use a smoking taper.

Every room has gaps that let in cold air and let out your expensive heat. You'll be surprised at the ease with which most of these annoying and wasteful draughts can be eliminated.

Warm air escaping up chimney

You can use a lighted candle instead, but be very careful with the naked flame, especially near curtains.

Your house will probably have some draught excluders already, but remember that most have a limited life and check your old ones for effectiveness while you are thinking about the new ones. Make a mental note to do an annual check in future.

A smoking taper helps you to detect draughts around doors and windows.

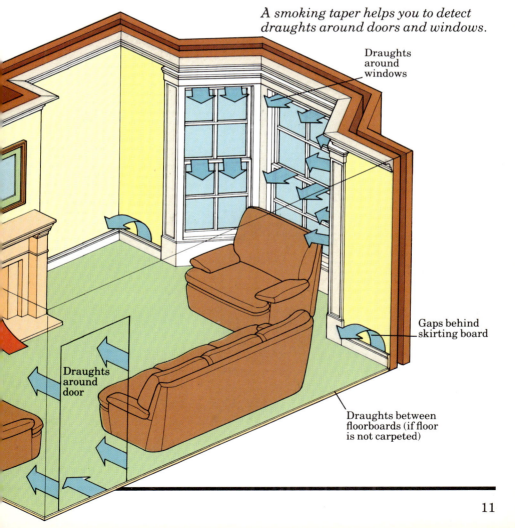

Draughts around windows

Gaps behind skirting board

Draughts around door

Draughts between floorboards (if floor is not carpeted)

DOORS AND WINDOWS

It's the gaps around the opening parts of external doors and windows that let in most draughts. With windows, one solution, if you never open the window and cannot foresee a need to open it in the future, is to paint the opening part shut by letting paint dribble into the gap until it is sealed. But there won't be many windows you can treat like this and for the others and for doors you will need proper weather-stripping. There is a large choice, much of which is self-adhesive and therefore very easy to fit.

Broadly speaking, it pays to buy the most durable weatherstripping you can afford. Although the longer-lasting types are more expensive to buy in the first place, they usually work out cheaper in the long run.

For windows that are rarely opened, use liquid draught seal. It can be peeled off when not required. Below: a porch reduces the heat lost through an exterior door.

PORCHES

Porches help to windproof an external door as well as providing a winter home for tender plants and a place for outdoor gear. If possible, have the porch door at right angles to the front door to make a better wind break. In houses where there is no possibility of a porch on the outside of the house,

A conservatory that encloses rear doors or windows reduces heat loss, and adds an extra room to your home.

consider instead an inner lobby with glazed doors. At the back of the house the back door or french windows can be given similar treatment by a lean-to greenhouse or a conservatory.

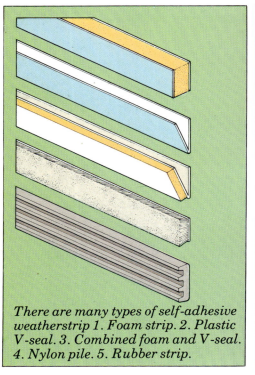

There are many types of self-adhesive weatherstrip 1. Foam strip. 2. Plastic V-seal. 3. Combined foam and V-seal. 4. Nylon pile. 5. Rubber strip.

Start by cleaning the paintwork thoroughly using sugar soap.

Start at the top of the frame, pressing the sticky side firmly in position.

Trim the corners neatly ensuring that there are no gaps left.

All self-adhesive weatherstripping is fitted to the window or door *frame* in a position where the window or door will compress it when closed.

Before you fit the weatherstripping you need to ensure that the surface is clean enough for the adhesive to stick well. Wipe the surface with a damp cloth and leave it to dry. If you are decorating, it's a good idea to add weatherstripping to your list of tasks to do.

Most self-adhesive weatherstripping has a protective backing paper to stop the layers sticking on the roll. Peel off approximately 100mm of the backing and starting at the top of the frame, press the sticky side of the tape

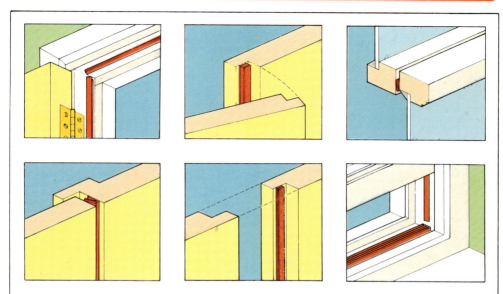

Whenever possible fit weather-stripping to the frames of doors or windows. In some positions any of the types shown will work, but care is needed with sliding surfaces to ensure a lasting draughtproof fit.

into position. Moving downwards, gradually peel off the backing paper and press the tape in place. Cut the roll with scissors when you get to the bottom.

Foam strip is a squashy foam usually with a washable surface. It's the cheapest weatherstripping you can buy, but lasts only a few years. Good for sealing around interior doors, it shouldn't be your first choice for windows or exterior doors.

Plastic V-seal is a pre-scored strip of plastic which you fold to make a V. It's a medium-priced and versatile weatherstripping which can cope with a wide range of gap sizes. Although the plastic can become brittle with age, it is guaranteed for five years.

Combined foam and V-seal is foam strip welded to a plastic V-seal to give a double-action weatherstripping. It's more expensive than ordinary foam strip, and has the same limitations.

Rubber strip is a hard-wearing, weather-resistant, weatherstripping suitable for gaps from 1.5mm to 2.5mm wide. It's one of the more expensive self-adhesive weatherstrippings, but it's guaranteed to last at least five years.

Nylon pile is a brush pile weatherstripping and the only self-adhesive type that can be used on sliding windows, as well as hinged ones. It's the most expensive self-adhesive weatherstripping, again guaranteed to last five years.

OTHER TYPES

Reusable tubular strip is a rubbery tube which you simply tuck into the gap. It holds itself in place and can easily be removed when you want to open the door or window. It is suitable for gaps up to 3mm wide and especially recommended for patio doors. It can be reused again and again.

Draught seal could be the answer for windows that you don't open very often. It's a clear liquid which you squeeze out of a tube to fill the gap. Easy to use, it dries to an unobtrusive rubbery bead which can be peeled off when you want to open the window or redecorate.

Brush strip is' perhaps the most durable weatherstripping and also the most expensive. It's screwed in place on the inside of the window frame so that the bristles cover the gap and rest against the window itself.

Sash windows
The sliding action of sash windows means that they need special weatherstripping. At the top and the bottom you can use almost any type of weatherstripping. For where the windows meet in the middle use either V-seal or self-adhesive brush pile. For the sides use brush strip or V-seal. If you won't want to open the window, use reusable tubular seal or draught seal.

Metal windows
The usual problem here is that the gap is too narrow to accommodate the bulkier types of weatherstripping. For windows you want to open try V-seal; if you won't open the window, at least in the winter months, use draught seal.

French windows
If there is a rebate where the two windows meet, you should be able to use any of the self-adhesive strips. If there is no rebate, use V-seal or self-adhesive brush pile.

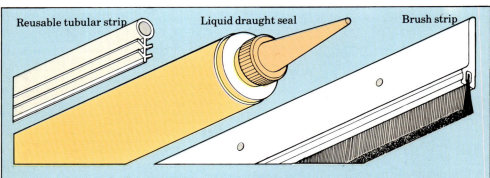

Reusable tubular strip   Liquid draught seal   Brush strip

There are several types of draught proofing material for special purposes. Tubular strip simply tucks into any gap. Liquid draught seal is useful for windows that are rarely opened. Brush strip is expensive but durable.

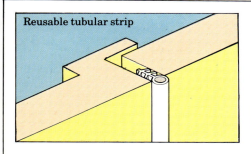

Reusable tubular strip

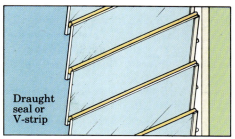

Draught seal or V-strip

Re-usable tubular strip is made of rubber and simply tucks into a gap for instant draught proofing.

Louvre windows are difficult to draught proof, although V-strip should work on the edges.

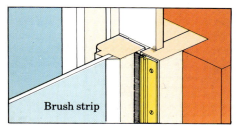

Brush strip

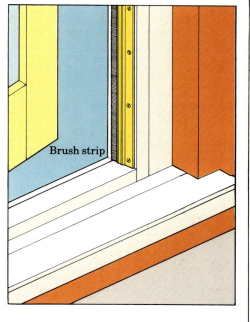

Brush strip

Sash windows can be draught proofed with V-strip, but must be dismantled. Brush strip is a good alternative.

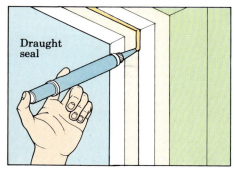

Draught seal

If you have windows that are rarely opened, liquid draught seal is a simple, method of draught proofing.

Although brush strip is the most expensive type of weatherstripping, it is very durable and versatile. Ensure that it is positioned so that the bristles are in firm contact with the surface to eliminate gaps.

UNDER DOORS

The gap under a door can be dealt with by fitting some sort of flap to the bottom of the door or by fitting a threshold excluder to the floor under the door. There are also combination excluders which have one part fitted to the door and another to the floor.

You normally choose one of these for an interior door. There are several different types:

Plain excluders have some sort of flexible seal that touches the floor and covers the gap. They're easy to fit and can be stuck or screwed in place. Brush excluders are the commonest type. They are suitable for hinged or sliding doors.

Flap excluders are an alternative, but only for hinged doors. Brush and flap excluders both drag across the floor when the door is opened.

Automatic flap excluders solve the dragging problem by having a flap which lifts as the door is opened and drops back as the door is closed. They cost more than ordinary flap excluders, but should last longer.

Floor dogs were once a common sight in most homes. They make good draught excluders for internal doors, provided you make a point of always replacing them after the door has been opened. Heavy ones filled with sand are better than those filled with lighter stuffings.

THRESHOLD EXCLUDERS

Threshold excluders for exterior doors help to keep out the weather and dust from the street as well as draughts. Most are screwed into place and are therefore easier to fit if the door sill is wooden. Before you buy a threshold excluder, make sure that it will fit the gap beneath your door. Check also that the sill is flat and the bottom of the door is straight – if it isn't it may need planing.

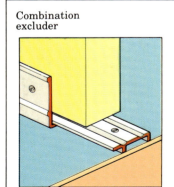

Combination excluder

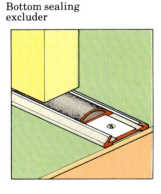

Bottom sealing excluder

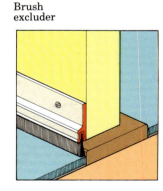

Brush excluder

There are many types of draught excluder for the gaps under doors.

They range in cost and complexity from a simple brush strip to combination

Bottom-sealing excluders work by filling the gap from underneath, usually with a dome of plastic which is compressed by the door as it closes.

Face-sealing excluders bridge the gap with an upstanding bar which seals on to the outside face of the door when it is closed. Some are supplied in kits with a weatherbar. If your door hasn't got a weatherbar and the excluder doesn't come with one, buy one separately otherwise water will be able to drip behind the excluder.

Combination excluders have two parts which mate to form the seal. One part is fitted to the door, the other to the floor.

Replacement sill excluders usually incorporate a bottom seal and a face seal. They are expensive and can be tricky to fit, but worth considering if your existing sill is in poor condition and needs replacement.

Brush strip excluders are simple to fit. The bristles are flexible enough for good contact on uneven floors.

Replacement
sill excluder

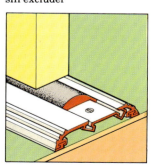

Face sealing
excluder

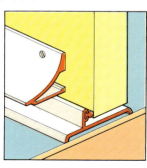

Automatic
brush excluder

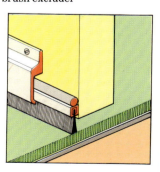

and replacement sill excluders. Check the gap under your door before buying

a bottom-sealing excluder to ensure that there is sufficient space.

Cat flap

Weatherstrip

Other gaps

For letterboxes Fit a letter box seal. Most have a covering flap over two brush seals. The brushes meet around anything put through the letterbox to stop draughts even if something is left partway through.

For loft hatches Fit self-adhesive strip all the way round the ledge against which the hatch door closes. If your hatch opens down to make way for a loft ladder, make sure there is a strong catch holding the hatch door tightly enough to compress the strip.

Some types of cat flap have integral weatherstripping. If not, ensure that the movement of the flap is not affected when you fit it.

For gaps around pipes going through the ceiling Use caulking strips. They're flexible enough to fill any shape of gap.

For fireplaces Fit a throat restrictor in the narrowest part of the chimney or have a piece of board which you slide across the top of the fireplace when it is not in use.

Letterbox seals are a quick and easy way to solve a draughty letterbox.

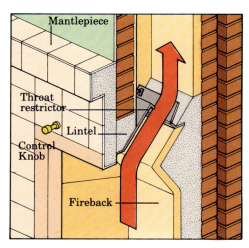

Mantlepiece

Throat restrictor

Lintel

Control Knob

Fireback

A fireplace fitted with a throat restrictor, stops heat loss up the chimney, when the fire is not in use.

Don't forget to weatherstrip the loft hatch and fit a strong catch to ensure a firm draughtpoof seal.

It's important not to stop all your home's natural ventilation. For one thing your house will become stuffy; more seriously there is a risk that there will not be enough air left to supply fuel-burning appliances such as gas fires and boilers. Any heater which burns with a flame needs air to keep going. If it is starved of air, it won't burn properly and the toxic gases it produces will not be able to escape quickly enough – with possibly fatal results.

A room containing a boiler must have a permanent ventilation opening, such as an airbrick, which must not be blocked. In rooms containing fixed heaters or portable ones – such as LPG heaters – do not draughtproof the door to the rest of the house.

CONDENSATION
One unexpected drawback of stopping up the gaps around your house is that you may suddenly start to suffer from condensation. Most homes suffer from condensation at some time or other. It appears when warm air which contains a lot of water vapour meets a cold surface such as a window pane. Controlling condensation means striking a balance between:

- ventilation – to remove damp air

- heating – because warm air can hold more moisture than cold air, and warm surfaces are less condensation prone

- insulation – mainly because it helps to make the most of the heating, but also in some situations because it raises the temperature of cold, condensation-prone, surfaces.

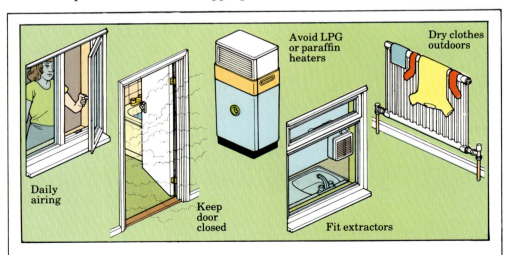

Avoid LPG or paraffin heaters

Dry clothes outdoors

Daily airing

Keep door closed

Fit extractors

There are many ways to avoid condensation. Keep kitchen and bathroom doors shut and give your home a daily airing.

It is important to try to maintain a balance between the heating, ventilation and insulation in your home.

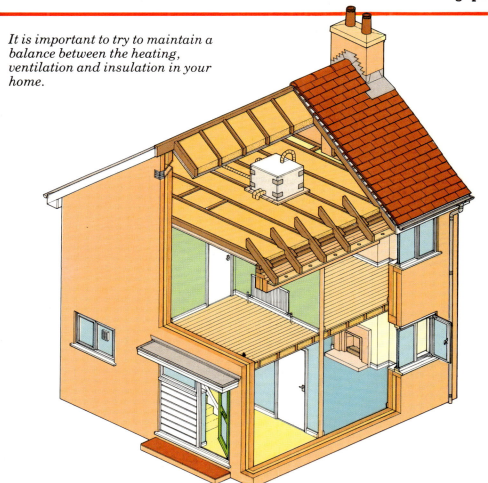

Unfortunately, draughtproofing improves the insulation at the expense of the ventilation and frequently upsets the balance.

If you've got a lot of condensation, there are some simple things you can do to relieve the problem:

- give the house a daily airing to clear out all the damp air. Do it by opening all the windows for ten minutes or so every morning

- dry clothes out of doors or in a tumble drier which is vented to the outside
- keep kitchen and bathroom doors shut when you are cooking or washing and fit extractor fans in these rooms to draw away the damp air
- avoid using portable LPG or paraffin heaters – these generate large amounts of water vapour.

Loft insulation

Insulating a loft is a relatively quick and easy job, with potentially large heat savings. If you had no insulation in your roof before, you will immediately notice the difference in warmer upstairs temperatures as well as lower fuel bills. And it isn't an expensive insulating job, especially if you qualify for a grant under the Government's Home Insulation Scheme of two-thirds the cost.

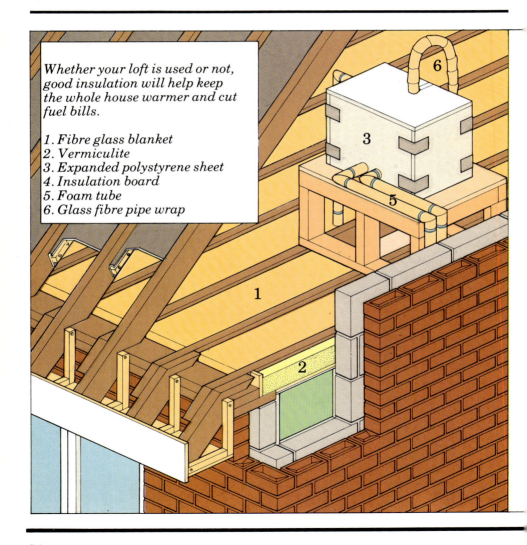

Whether your loft is used or not, good insulation will help keep the whole house warmer and cut fuel bills.

1. Fibre glass blanket
2. Vermiculite
3. Expanded polystyrene sheet
4. Insulation board
5. Foam tube
6. Glass fibre pipe wrap

The main choices for insulating a loft are glass fibre blanket which is supplied in rolls 100mm and 150mm thick and 350mm wide, or a loose-fill material such as vermiculite. Glass fibre blanket is the more widely available and popular of the two and is a little cheaper to use.

Expanded polystyrene sheet is use-ful for awkward places where neither of the other materials can easily be fitted, and for insulating cold water cisterns.

If you're planning to have the work done for you there is a further option of mineral wool fibre which can be blown into your loft by a contractor.

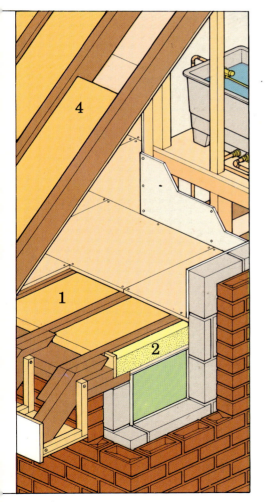

Glass fibre blanket is, by far, the most popular loft insulation material.

Before you start

Working in the loft space isn't difficult, but it is dirty and as there are no floorboards you must equip yourself with a sturdy platform to work from. A good light to work by and to show you were to put your feet is another essential. Prepare for laying your insulation by:

● making sure you have a safe way of climbing in and out of the loft – a proper loft ladder, which folds back into the loft when not in use, is best. Next best is a ladder which will reach right up into the loft hatch, one part of a long extension ladder, for instance. A stepladder which leaves you to scramble the last few feet isn't a good choice, but

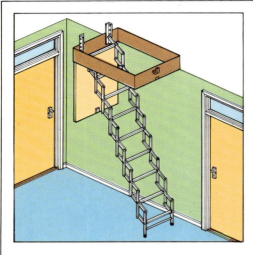

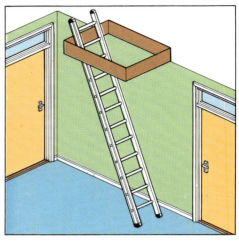

An extending loft ladder is the safest and most convenient method of access to your roof space.

A sectional extension ladder is the next best choice. Always ensure it is secured firmly.

A hook-on lamp provides good light for working. Clip-on lamps may not

have jaws wide enough for rafters, so nail on some lengths of batten.

A step ladder is seldom tall enough for easy access. Get a helper to hold it steady or tie it securely.

Use a plank or two for a working platform in the loft — this is far safer than balancing on the joists.

if you have no alternative, tie the stepladder firmly in place or have someone holding it when you go up or down.

- equipping yourself with at least one strong plank or board a metre or so long, to kneel on as you work. If you have more planks, you could use them to make a walkway across the loft.

It's a good idea to inspect your roof before you lay insulation. Look particularly at:

- **the roof timbers** – check that they are in good condition; that there are no signs of rot or woodworm. Check for signs of damp and look for any chinks in the roof covering which will show you where water is

getting in. Put right any defects before you insulate.

- **the wiring** – electric cables to the upstairs lights normally run through the loft. The insulation shouldn't cover existing wiring, so check that there is enough slack in the cables to allow you to tuck your insulation under them. If the wiring is the old rubber-covered type, now is the time to consider having it renewed.

- **the plumbing** – take the opportunity to check that cisterns and pipes are in good condition before wrapping them in insulation.

- **the ventilation** – when you have insulated your loft it will become much colder and there is a risk of condensation if the space isn't adequately ventilated. If the roof is felted or boarded under the tiles, you will need ventilation at the eaves. Gaps at the eaves through which you can see more or less continuous daylight, will be providing sufficient ventilation. If there are no gaps, look for separate ventilators elsewhere. If there are none, you will have to sort the ventilation out before you insulate.

Ventilation can be provided by drilling 50mm diameter holes at 200mm intervals in the soffit board on the two long sides of the roof. Block the holes with wire netting to stop birds and squirrels getting in.

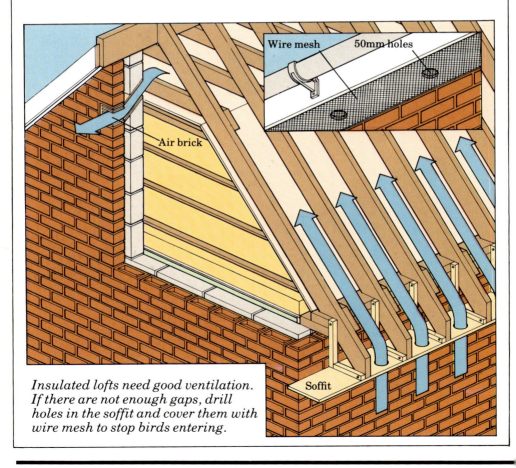

Wire mesh   50mm holes

Air brick

Soffit

Insulated lofts need good ventilation. If there are not enough gaps, drill holes in the soffit and cover them with wire mesh to stop birds entering.

MEASURING UP

If you want to be precise about measuring up, you need to get into the loft, count the number of spaces between joists and measure the length of each joist run across the roof. Then multiply these two figures together to get the total length of insulation needed to cover the loft floor completely.

A less precise, but easier, way is to measure the length and width of your loft space and calculate its area. Measuring the outside walls at ground level is the easiest way to do this. Divide the loft area by the area that a pack of insulation will cover to get the number of rolls you will need.

A twin pack of 100mm covers 3.2 square metres, a twin pack of 150mm covers 2.4 square metres, assuming

The R value is shown clearly on packs of insulation material.

that your joists are 350mm apart. Don't worry if your joists are closer than this, simply tuck the insulation in to make a small curve. It will cost you a little more to do your loft, but you'll have put in more insulation.

Don't be surprised if your sums work out to what seems a large number of rolls; the average house is going to need around 15 twin packs. You won't of course be able to get this many rolls in your car in one trip, so enquire about delivery services.

R VALUES

On the packing of your rolls of insulation, you will find a number called an R value. This is a measure of the effectiveness of the insulation. The higher the R value, the better the insulator. R value is directly proportional to thickness so 100mm glass fibre blanket has an R value of 2.5; 150mm has an R value of 3.75.

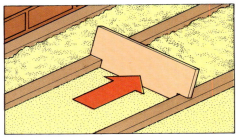

There are certain situations where a loose fill insulation material, such as vermiculite, may be an advantage. It is simple to use; you just pour it *between the joists and level off with a piece of wood. A depth of 100mm to 150mm will provide good insulation and help reduce heating bills.*

LAYING YOUR INSULATION

You may find that handling glass fibre irritates your skin. Wear smooth clothing which will not pick up fibres, tuck your trousers into socks and wear rubber gloves with your sleeves tucked into these. It's a good idea to wear a dust mask too. When you have finished, rinse your skin thoroughly by taking a shower to float the fibres off. Don't rub your skin.

Put your kneeling board across

When laying glass fibre blanket, wear a mask and gloves. Use planks for a safe working platform.

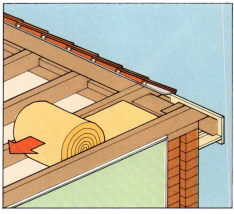

Start from the eaves, allow 50mm for ventilation. Cut in the middle of the loft and start from the opposite side.

joists at a place close to the eaves. Place the roll of insulation in the space between joists to one side of you and starting just short of the eaves, to give the necessary gap for ventilation, unroll the insulation towards the centre of the loft. Cut the roll at the centre of the loft and start again at the opposite side of the loft.

The gap that is left at the eaves for ventilation needs to be at least 50mm wide. Cutting the end of the mat at an angle helps to achieve this.

As you work, remember that the insulation must not cover electric wiring. Cut the insulation if necessary and use a stick to push it under the wires. Be careful not to pull or stretch them. If there are any light fittings recessed into the ceiling, stop the insulation short on either side of the fitting.

Do not forget to insulate the loft

hatch door. The insulation will need to be tied in place. Garden netting or simply a criss-cross of string will do. Remember also to weatherstrip the hatch – see page 21.

Glass fibre blanket can be cut easily with a pair of heavy duty scissors.

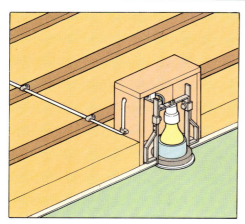

Blanket should not be laid over electrical wiring or light fittings in the ceiling, as it can cause overheating.

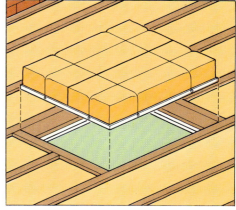

Remember that the loft hatch should also be insulated. Use garden netting or a criss-cross of string or tape.

Loft insulation

Warmth from below will help to keep the cold water storage cistern from freezing, so unless it is situated well above the joists, do not take insulation under the cistern. Do, however insulate round and over the cistern. The easiest way to do this is to wrap lengths of blanket around the cistern and secure them with string or tape. Make a proper cover for the top and take the precaution of wrapping it in stout paper or plastic so that there is no risk of fibres getting into the water.

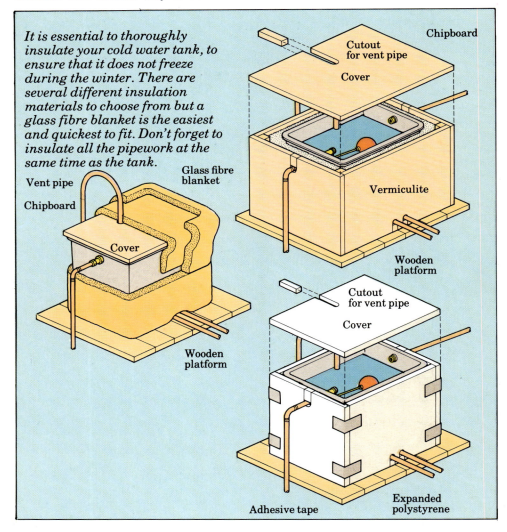

It is essential to thoroughly insulate your cold water tank, to ensure that it does not freeze during the winter. There are several different insulation materials to choose from but a glass fibre blanket is the easiest and quickest to fit. Don't forget to insulate all the pipework at the same time as the tank.

Chipboard

Cutout for vent pipe

Cover

Vent pipe

Glass fibre blanket

Chipboard

Cover

Vermiculite

Wooden platform

Wooden platform

Cutout for vent pipe

Cover

Adhesive tape

Expanded polystyrene

PIPES

You may well have been able to insulate some pipes as you installed the loft insulation; those that are above the level of the joist must also be done – including overflows. If you've any glass fibre blanket insulation left over, you can cut it into strips and wrap it bandage fashion around the pipes, securing the ends with string or tape. You can get purpose-made strips of glass fibre too. Plastic foam tube split lengthways so that you can fit it over the pipe makes a neat job. It's easier than glass fibre to fit around pipes which don't have much space behind them. Some types have a zip-close fastener, others have to be stuck or taped in place around bends. For wrapping up the body of stop valves, glass fibre strips are best.

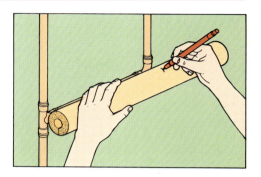

Measure each length of foam tube carefully and mark with a felt tip pen.

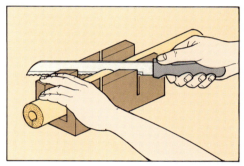

For neat corners use a mitre box and a fine toothed saw or sharp knife.

Whilst foam tube is best for straight pipes, this self-adhesive strip makes wrapping joints and stop cocks simple.

Some types of foam tube will need to be taped at joints and corners.

PROBLEM ROOFS

If you live in a chalet-style house with upstairs rooms set into the roof space, there will be parts of your roof which cannot be insulated by laying insulation between the joists. The solution is to install insulation against the underside of the roof, between the rafters. But this needs to be done with care to minimise the risk of condensation developing behind the insulation material.

If you have access to the underside of the roof, arrange the insulation so that there is a clear gap of 50mm between the insulation and the underside of the roof. Ensure that this gap is ventilated from the eaves.

Cover the insulation with a layer of plastic sheet which is well lapped and taped at the joints to stop moisture getting through. Fit ceiling boards over the top.

If your rafters are already boarded in, you may still be able to insulate by sliding rigid insulating boards down from the top of the gap where it is open in the loft. Choose boards which are thin enough to leave the necessary gap for ventilation.

FLAT ROOFS

The risk of condensation is even more serious with a flat roof. If you make any attempt to insulate, by sliding in rigid insulation boards or by fitting a new insulated ceiling beneath the existing one. It is essential to provide ventilation and to incorporate a plastic sheet as a vapour barrier.

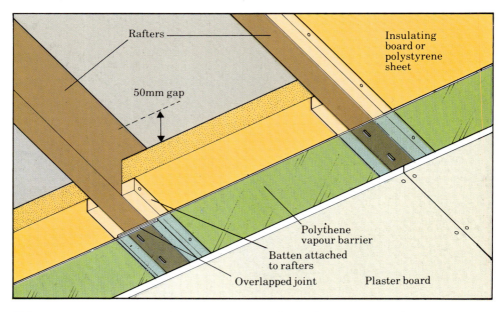

Where rooms are set into the roofspace, you need to insulate between the rafters. Ensure a gap of 50mm between insulation material and roof.

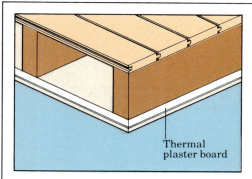

In a flat roofed extension, the ceiling can be insulated with thermal plasterboard, with a layer of polystyrene. This is only economical if the ceiling needs replacement.

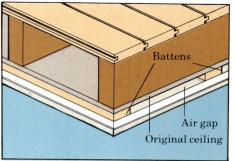

If the ceiling is high, a false ceiling incorporating insulation could be suspended beneath it. In both cases a vapour barrier and adequate ventilation are essential.

GOVERNMENT HOME INSULATION SCHEME

Under the Government's Homes Insulation Scheme 1984, you may be able to get a grant to help towards the cost of insulating your loft.

To qualify for a grant, there can be no existing insulation more than 30mm thick in any part of the loft, and there must not previously have been any thicker insulation.

You will not qualify for a grant if your home was built after 1975; if a grant has already been paid towards loft insulation; for lofts over rooms used solely for business or storage; or for flat roofs.

The grant is currently 66% of the cost up to a maximum of £69 for most people, but elderly or severely disabled applicants on low incomes may qualify for a higher grant of 90% or £99 whichever is the least.

Make enquiries about grants to your local authority. They will ask you to fill in an application form. You must not start work until you have the go-ahead and you must use an approved material on the local authority's list. (Texas Loft insulation is an approved material.)

When the work is done you fill in another form to claim your grant. To be able to claim your grant you must not only have insulated the loft itself, but also any cisterns and water pipes in the loft, and your hot water storage cylinder.

Insulating walls

Although a lot of heat is lost through walls, insulating them is not usually a do-it-yourself job and it is relatively expensive. However, once you've tackled the priority jobs, it is well worth turning your attention to your walls, for insulated walls not only save money, but are also more comfortable to live with.

Before you can decide how to insulate your house walls you need to know how they are built. If the house is brick and the outside walls have a lot of end-on bricks showing – as in the drawing – it is most likely that the walls are solid brick. Find out how wide the walls are by measuring the thickness at a doorway.

If your outside brick walls have no end-on bricks visible, or only a few, then your walls are probably cavity construction – where the wall is built up from the foundations in two independent leaves linked every so often by metal ties. The inside leaf of a

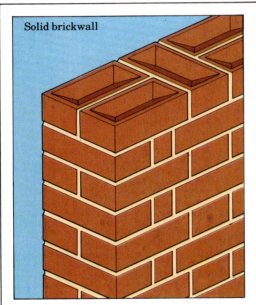

Solid brickwall

You can usually recognise solid brick walls by the number of end-on bricks that are visible. If measured at a doorway, solid walls are usually about 230mm thick.

Cavity brickwall

Cavity walls have no end-on bricks showing, or very few. They are also usually thicker than solid walls. Whether bricks or blocks they are suitable for insulation.

cavity wall can be brick, block or timber frame. Both brick and block walls can usually be insulated by filling the cavity with insulation; the cavity in timber-frame walls should not be filled under any circumstances.

You'll probably know if your house is timber frame. It will be a fairly new house and there may be a notice near to the house fuse box or in the airing cupboard which tells that the walls are timber frame. You may be able to tell timber-frame walls by tapping them on the inside – a hollow sound is the clue. Timber-frame walls incorpo-

rate a high degree of insulation, so it is no disadvantage.

Stone walls may be cavity construction or solid. Most are not suitable for cavity insulation.

CAVITY WALL INSULATION
With cavity wall insulation the insulation is introduced into the wall through holes drilled in the outer leaf. It's a job for a contractor with the appropriate materials and equipment and can never be d-i-y. There are three main materials which can be used to fill the cavity.

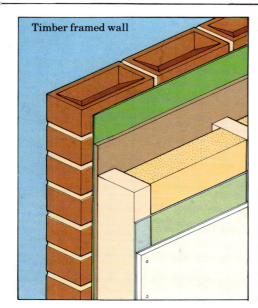

Timber framed wall

Timber framed walls, which often have an outer brick skin, are usually well insulated already. If you are unsure, tap the inside wall which should sound hollow if timber framed.

Solid stone wall

Stone walls may be solid or built with a cavity. In either case they are unsuitable for insulation although they could be insulated inside or on the exterior. (see pages 42/43)

- **urea-formaldehyde foam** is a foamed plastic which is injected in as a wet foam and 'cures' in the cavity.

- **expanded polystyrene beads** are tiny plastic pellets which are blown into the cavity. The beads some installers use have a coating of adhesive which dries to bond the beads together.

- **mineral wool fibre** is finely spun glass or rock fibre which is blown into the cavity to form a mat of insulation.

WHICH TO CHOOSE?

U-f foam is the cheapest cavity wall insulation, but despite this it may not to be your best choice, for unless the insulation is installed very carefully into a wall which has been checked and found free of defects, there can be problems. Fumes with a distinctive odour are given off as the foam cures. Some people find this irritating, and there is concern that the fumes could be injurious to health. If a problem does arise with u-f foam insulation, it is difficult and expensive to remove the foam. It isn't easy with the other materials either – but it is possible.

If you decide to use u-f foam, choose an installer who is registered under the British Standards Institute surveillance scheme. This is your guarantee that the firm will comply with the British Standards dealing with the installation of u-f foam. There are two: BS 5617 for the u-f foam itself and BS 5618 dealing with its installation.

If you choose one of the other materials, ask the installer whether he has a current British Board of Agrement (BBA) certificate. This will confirm that the BBA has tested and approved the product for cavity fill. Ask to see the certificate as it may have restrictions on the use of the insulation in certain types of housing.

Your installer will need to give the building control department of your local authority notice of his intention to fill your walls and the local authority will look for one of these two types of certification.

Holes are drilled at intervals in the wall prior to the injection of the insulation material.
The insulating material is injected into the cavity via a hose. The material can be u-f foam, polystyrene beads, or mineral wool fibre.

CHECKS BEFORE FILLING

Your installer should check that your walls are in a fit condition to be filled, but it does no harm to make your own checks. Look out for:

- patches of penetrating damp seen as spoilt decorations on the inside

- damaged mortar between bricks on the outside wall

- damaged rendering

- openings where the cavity opens into the loft space or an eaves cupboard – there should be bricks closing the top, but they are sometimes omitted

- holes in the wall through which the foam could get into the house – there may be holes around pipes or vents passing through the wall.

RADIATORS

Central heating radiators are often installed on outside walls and some of their heat goes straight out through the wall. You can reduce the heat lost by half by lining the wall behind the radiator with reflecting foil.

Measure the foil against the radiator and trim to size.

Checks after filling

Again the installer should make his own checks. Before he goes try to make sure that there has been no spillage into the house. Switch off the electricity and look behind sockets installed on outside walls, these can sometimes fill up with foam. Check that the airbricks for underfloor ventilation are clear.

If you have had cavity wall insulation installed, check the following: airbricks are clear, electrical sockets on external walls have no foam inside and no foam has leaked where pipework pierces the extenal walls.

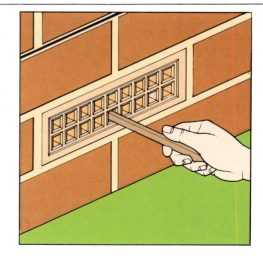

Most purpose-made radiator foils are supplied with self-adhesive pads which you use to stick them to the wall behind the radiator. It can be tricky to tuck the foil behind the radiator, but you can get round this by sticking the foil to a piece of hardboard cut to fit over the radiator wall brackets.

If there is enough space above the radiator, consider fitting a radiator shelf. This will deflect more heat into the room and prevent dust carried in the rising air from soiling the wall.

Fix the foil in position on the wall using the self-adhesive pads.

Replace the radiator on its brackets and reconnect the pipework.

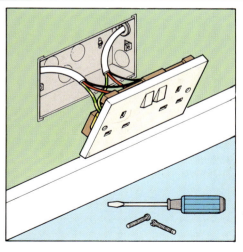

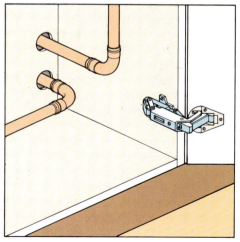

SOLID WALLS

Insulating solid walls is neither easy nor cheap and the question of whether it is worth doing depends very much on how long you plan to live in your home. It also depends on how thick your solid walls are. Walls only 9in (225mm) wide will be losing heat quite fast, whereas walls 13½in (330mm) or more thick lose their heat fractionally more slowly than a typically unfilled cavity wall. Clearly if

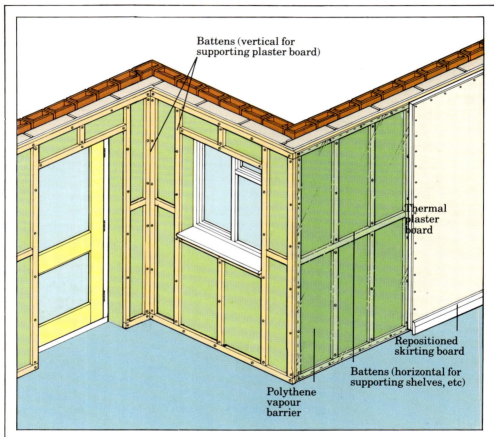

Battens (vertical for supporting plaster board)

Thermal plaster board

Repositioned skirting board

Battens (horizontal for supporting shelves, etc)

Polythene vapour barrier

Installing internal insulation consists of mounting thermal plasterboard on a framework of battens. You must always fit a vapour barrier of polythene sheeting with lapped and taped joints to stop moisture getting through. It is also necessary to move skirting boards, radiators, electric switches and sockets, and possibly door and window frames.

you live in a detached house with a large area of outside wall, insulation will be more worthwhile than if you live in a terraced house.

You can insulate a solid wall on the inside or the outside. Internal insulation has the advantage that you can do a room at a time and concentrate on the rooms you heat the most. It can be a d-i-y job and it can therefore be cheaper than external insulation. However it makes rooms smaller and, although fixing the insulation isn't difficult, skirting boards, radiators, electric sockets and switches, and door and window frames may all have to be moved. External insulation causes no disruption inside the house, but because it adds to the thickness of walls there are still problems with moving things – drain pipes for instance. It is expensive and normally worth considering only if you need to have work done to the outside of the house for other reasons – if the existing rendering needs attention for instance, it may be worth opting for a new insulating render. Some types of external insulation change the outside appearance of your wall and you may need to obtain planning permission to use them.

HOW IT'S DONE
Internal wall insulation is normally installed by fitting a framework of timber battens to the wall, with insulation between the battens, and plasterboard or wallboards on top. To stop moisture getting behind the framework and condensing there with subsequent damp problems, a sheet of plastic must be sandwiched between the insulation and the boards.

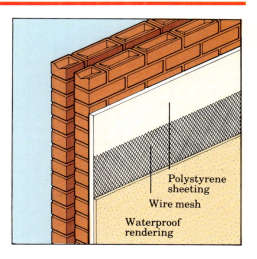

Polystyrene sheeting

Wire mesh

Waterproof rendering

EXTERNAL INSULATION
There are several different external insulation systems. The drawing shows a typical one using waterproof rendering, keyed to metal mesh, over a layer of polystyrene.

EXPANDED POLYSTYRENE
Where your walls are cold to touch and it is difficult or beyond your means to install wall insulation, lining them with expanded polystyrene can make them feel a little warmer. Expanded polystyrene veneers for walls are typically about 5mm thick which is enough to take the chill off the wall, although not nearly enough to count as insulation.

You buy expanded polystyrene on the roll 595mm wide, and hang it much like wallpaper in vertical lengths using a special adhesive. The veneer can be papered or painted over, but it is important to use only water-based paint such as vinyl emulsion. Note that this also applies to expanded polystyrene ceiling tiles.

Ceiling insulation

Ceilings don't normally need to be insulated, heat from downstairs rooms will help to heat the rooms above and upstairs ceilings are usually insulated from above. In rooms, however, where there is no access to the space above, it may be necessary to insulate from below.

The easiest and by far the cheapest way is to use expanded polystyrene ceiling tiles. They'll reduce by about a quarter the heat lost through a ceiling into an uninsulated roof. Tiles are available in three sizes: 300mm square; 406mm square and 500mm square. There are plain tiles and moulded tiles with surface designs.

For fire precautions, it is important that tiles are stuck firmly to the ceiling. Wash the surface well and scrape off any loose paint, plaster or paper. If it is gloss paint, rub it down with abrasive paper. Coat a new ceiling with dilute wallpaper adhesive. Spread the special adhesive liberally over the entire back of the tile, taking care not to get any on the front. An offcut of wood makes a useful tool to save indentations in the tiles when you press them into place. If you're going to paint the tiled ceiling, you'll find it much easier to do if you paint the tiles before sticking them up. Again for precaution against fire hazards, use only water-based paint. Polystyrene coving makes a neat edging to a tiled ceiling.

Another way to insulate a ceiling is to fix plasterboard with expanded polystyrene backing over the existing ceiling. This 'thermal' plasterboard can be nailed directly into the ceiling joists using long plasterboard nails – use a gimlet or bradawl to find the joist positions. The cracks and joints between boards are filled with jointing tape and filler. Plaster coving makes a neat finish round the perimeter.

A tongued and grooved timber ceiling can be installed with insulation behind if long battens are first screwed to the undersides of the ceiling joists. The depth of the battens determines the thickness of insulation – allow at least 50mm. Nail polythene sheet to the battens to double as a vapour check and temporary support for the insulation. Nail the tongued and grooved boards to the battens using secret nailing, where each board hides the nails holding the previous one in place.

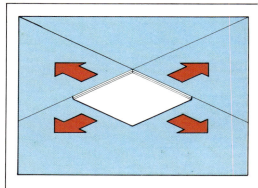

When preparing to apply polystyrene ceiling tiles, mark a centre point on the ceiling. This will ensure that the tiles are cut equally on either side.

A suspended metal grid ceiling can be fitted with special panels made of glass fibre with a washable surface to provide ceiling insulation.

A tongue and grooved timber ceiling can conceal an insulation layer. However, it is important to include a vapour check barrier.

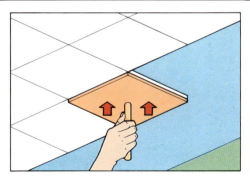

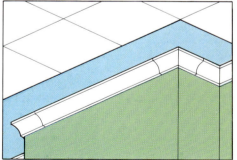

After spreading the special adhesive apply pressure evenly using a flat piece of wood with a dowel handle to avoid denting the tile surface.

However carefully you cut the edge tiles, the appearance will be improved by fitting coving. This must be cut in a mitre box for accurate corners.

Insulating floors

Insulating your floors can reduce the heat loss through them quite considerably, but unfortunately it's a job which will usually involve you in considerable upheaval and it is often worthwhile considering only for new floors or for floors which are undergoing major renovation. Nevertheless there are some simple things you can do and in downstairs rooms you heat a lot – a kitchen for example – you may find full insulation is worth the effort, cost and upheaval.

Ground floors are generally made of either solid concrete laid directly on the earth or wooden boards supported on timber joists. Of the two an existing timber floor is by far the easier to insulate.

INSULATING A WOODEN FLOOR

The cheapest method is to use glass fibre blanket fitted between the joists on a cradle of plastic garden netting stapled to the joists. An alternative is to screw battens to the joists to form ledges to support expanded polystyrene sheets.

Whichever method you choose, it is important to leave a gap of about 30mm between the floorboards and the insulation material.

If there is a crawl space beneath your timber floor, you will be able to fit the insulation from below, and thus save the bother of lifting the floorboards. It will however be a cramped and dusty job and most of the precautions you need to take when insulating a loft space will apply: if you are using glass fibre insulation, you'll need to wear gloves and a mask and tuck your trousers into socks and sleeves into the gloves; all pipes must be carefully lagged to protect them from freezing, and the insulation shouldn't cover wiring.

A lot of heat can be lost through gaps and cracks in wooden floors. Fitted floor coverings such as carpets

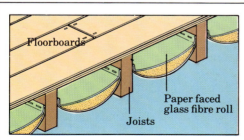

Paper faced glass fibre roll can be tacked or stapled between the joists for efficient underfloor insulation.

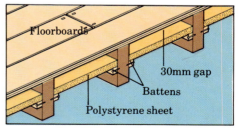

Polystyrene sheet will need battens to rest on. Allow a gap of at least 30mm to the underside of the floorboards.

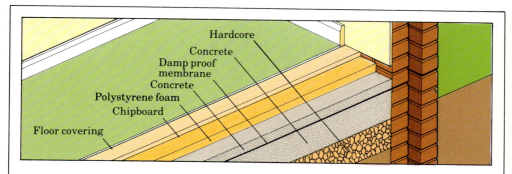

Hardcore
Concrete
Damp proof membrane
Concrete
Polystyrene foam
Chipboard
Floor covering

Insulating a solid floor when building an extension is fairly simple. The only way to insulate an existing solid floor, *is to put a new floor of chipboard 'floating' over a layer of expanded polystyrene.*

stop most draughts, but if you have a carpet square with bare boards around it, or if you have bare polished boards, you will need to block any gaps or cracks.

- Cover the gap between the floor and the skirting with quarter-circle wooden moulding pinned in place with a strip of self-adhesive foam excluder between the moulding and the floor.
- Fill holes around pipes or wires passing through the floor with flexible caulking.
- Fill gaps between boards which aren't the tongue and groove type with narrow timber strips tapped into place and planed off flush. If the floor surface will be hidden, use papier mache made by mixing shredded newspaper and wallpaper adhesive.

INSULATING A SOLID FLOOR

With an existing solid floor there is not a lot that you can do to stop the heat loss. One way is to construct a floating floor of expanded polystyrene slabs with a new chipboard floor over the top, but this is quite expensive and has several drawbacks. For one thing, the new floor will be higher than the old, so skirting boards will need to be moved and it will be necessary to shorten doors and fit a step to the floor in an adjacent room. For another, the new floor must incorporate a sealed layer of plastic sheet to stop moisture getting under the insulation.

Insulating a new concrete floor is a lot easier because the expanded polystyrene can be incorporated into the floor as it is constructed. It is normally placed between the concrete slab and the top screed. Another way to insulate a new floor is to lay the concrete over hollow clay blocks.

When this method is used the edge blocks are normally turned on their sides to give extra insulation to the edge of the floor where most of the heat is in fact lost.

Double glazing

Single-glazed windows lose heat very quickly and it can feel chilly to stand or sit by the cold expanse of glass. The solution is to double-glaze, but most double glazing is not cheap and it can take years for the savings in fuel bills to equal the cost of installing the double glazing. Nevertheless, double glazing will undoubtedly make your rooms seem warmer and you may be attracted by its other benefits such as cutting out noise.

A hinged double-glazing system is expensive to install, but allows easy access for ventilation and cleaning.

There are two main ways to double glaze: one is to install a second pane of glass (or plastic) in a separate frame behind the existing pane; the other is to replace the single pane of glass with a sealed unit which comprises two panes of glass sealed together.

Installing a second pane of glass is known as secondary double glazing. The second pane is normally installed on the inside of the existing window, although there are types intended for installation on the outside.

Secondary double glazing is usually

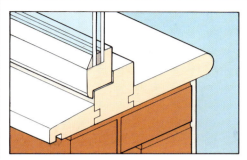

With sealed unit double-glazing, the original pane is replaced with a sealed unit of two panes incorporating an air-gap filled with dry air.

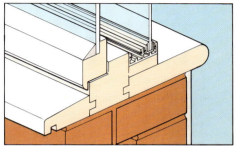

Secondary double-glazing usually consists of adding an additional pane of glass or plastic on the inside of the existing window frame.

cheaper than sealed unit double glazing and it has the advantage that you can have a wider air gap. There are many different types from inexpensive plastic film to fit yourself to sophisticated sliding systems with glass in aluminium frames which may be fitted DIY or be installed by a builder or window fitter.

Sealed units can be used to replace the single glazing in an existing frame, but they are more often installed as part of a complete replacement window. As well as plain glass units, there are ones made of obscured glass for use in bathrooms, leaded lights, stained glass designs, and small-paned Georgian styles. Units are also available with one pane of energy saving glass.

THE AIR GAP

The width of the air gap between the two glazing panes determines how well the double-glazed window will slow down the rate at which heat escapes. The optimum gap for good heat insulation is 20mm. If you want your double glazing to cut out noise, you need a gap as wide as you can manage – 100mm is often the most that you can have in the existing window reveal, but 150mm is better.

Sliding double-glazing systems can be fitted DIY or installed by a builder.

TYPES OF SECONDARY GLAZING

There are many types of secondary double-glazing available. They range in price, ease of fitting, efficiency and durability to suit all requirements.

Plastic film and double-sided tape

Double-sided self-adhesive tape goes on the window frame; the plastic film is stretched over the window and pressed on to the tape. The film is made taut and any wrinkles removed by heat from a hairdryer.

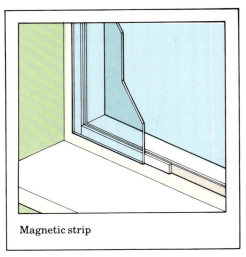
Magnetic strip

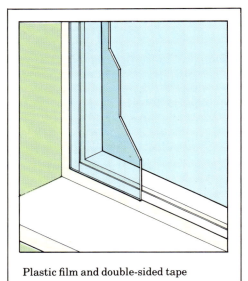
Plastic film and double-sided tape

Clip and screw channel

A flexible plastic channel pushes on to the glazing and is then fixed to the window frame with clips and screws. This system can be used wth either plastic sheet or glass and is removable for cleaning and ventilation..

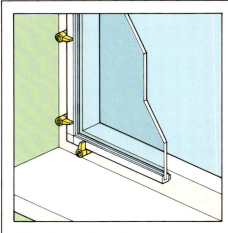
Clip and screw channel

Magnetic strip

A self-adhesive strip of steel goes on the window frame and a self-adhesive magnetic strip goes on the glazing. Magnetic attraction holds the glazing in place, but it can easily be removed for cleaning or in an emergency. It should be used with plastic sheet.

Hinged channel

A rigid plastic channel pushes on to the glazing to make a frame. On three sides a plain channel section is used; on the fourth side a special channel section incorporating a plastic strip is used to fix the frame to the window and make a hinge. The channel has integral weatherstripping to make a seal and turn clips are used as window catches. It is normally used with plastic sheet.

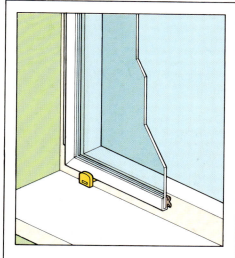

Hinged channel

Hinged frame

The glazing sits in a gasket and is framed by aluminium sections. Hinged panels are secured by hinges on one side and turn clips on the other three; fixed panels are held in place by turn clips. There is integral weatherstripping – usually a brush or tubular seal. It can be used with plastic sheet or glass.

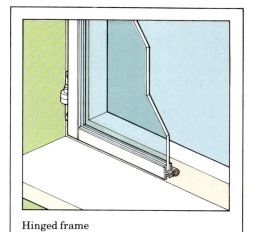

Hinged frame

Sliding systems

Horizontally sliding glazing is framed by a gasket and aluminium or plastic sections. It sits in a double track fitted to the window reveal, allowing ease of opening. The glazing can also be lifted from the frame for cleaning.

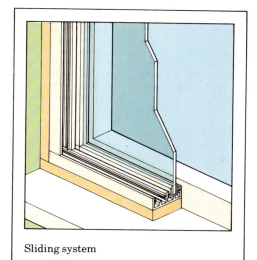

Sliding system

WHICH TO CHOOSE?

If your main reason for fitting double glazing is to save money on your heating bills, then choose the very cheapest system based on double-sided tape and plastic film. This should pay for itself in a couple of years. With all the other systems it will take several years for the savings on heating bills to recoup the cost.

Selecting between the other types of secondary glazing is largely a matter of looks and costs, but you need to consider whether a fixed system will suit you or if you will want to be able to open the window while the insulation is in place. Having windows that open is important not only for ventilation, but also for cleaning and, more importantly for escape in case of fire. Do not install fixed pane double-glazing on windows in upstairs rooms, unless it's a type such as magnetic tape which can be removed very easily and quickly – even by someone in a panic. Magnetic systems cannot be used on louvre windows or on roof lights or doors with glazed panels.

Fixed double-glazing which is screwed in place and strong hinged and sliding systems can help to make your windows more secure by acting as a burglar deterrent.

CONDENSATION

If moist air can get into the gap between the two panes of glazing, it may condense and cause misting on the outer pane, Fixed systems with a good seal on the inside are less prone to condensation. One solution if condensation is a nuisance is to drill holes to allow the moisture to drain from the cavity. Another is to put a

Heat shrink film is applied to the window frame with double-sided tape and shrunk taut with a hair dryer.

Flexible plastic film can be fixed with double-sided tape, as a quick and easy method of double-glazing. However it is prone to scratching.

container of silica gel crystals in the gap. These absorb moisture from the air and prevent it from condensing. When the crystals cease to be effective, they can be dried out in an oven.

Some systems use magnetic tape for holding light plastic glazing.

Condensation

Condensation is a common problem with double-glazing systems. It is caused by warm moist air condensing on the inside of the cold outer pane. If the system is fitted on a warm, dry day and there is a good inner seal, it is unlikely to be a problem.

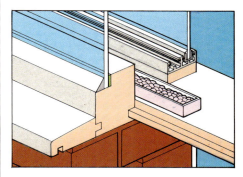

One way of avoiding condensation is to place a trough of silica gel crystals in the air-gap. They absorb moisture and can be dried in an oven.

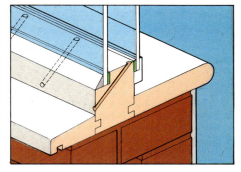

Holes can be drilled to allow moisture to escape. They should slope down towards the exterior of the frame to allow any excess water to drain away.

GLAZING MATERIALS

Of all the glazing materials you can use glass is the most durable. Glass is also relatively cheap, but it is because it is heavy it cannot be used with inexpensive secondary glazing tapes and frames and therefore often works out more expensive to use initially. Acrylic sheet is closest to glass for durability and looks, but it costs a little more a square metre.

Ordinary glass is clear to look through and, unless it is accidentally broken, it will last indefinitely without deteriorating. Glass 4mm thick is used for most windows, but large areas should be glazed with 6mm thick glass.

Safety glass costs considerably more than ordinary glass, but should be used for doors and low-level glazing. It can also be used for security. There are two types: toughened and laminated. Laminated glass can be cut to size by a glass merchant, but toughened glass has to be specially made to size in the factory.

Acrylic sheet is initially as clear as glass, but it tends to cloud a little as it ages. Like all plastics it tends to collect dust on its surface. It is tougher than glass and difficult to break, but can be scratched easily. It's commonly available 3mm or 4mm thick.

Polystyrene sheet is a cheaper type of plastic sheet which isn't as clear initially as acrylic and will deteriorate faster. If you use polystyrene double glazing, take it down in summer and store it away from light.

Plastic film is inexpensive and surprisingly clear. It can easily be damaged by sharp objects, so it isn't a good choice if you have pets with sharp claws. It will last longer if it is taken down in the summer. Store it in the dark and out of the reach of children.

FITTING SECONDARY GLAZING

Most secondary glazing is fitted on to the face of the existing window frame. The size of the air gap is then determined by the thickness of the window frame – it may be anything from a few millimetres on a metal-framed window to 50mm or more on a wooden window frame.

If you want a larger gap the glazing can be fitted to the sides of the window reveal, but, unless you are using a sliding system, this will entail making a frame of wooden battens.

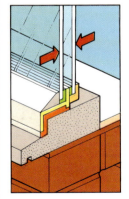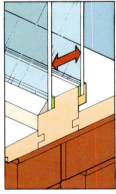

Ideally a air-gap of 20mm is needed to cut heat loss. On metal frames this may not be possible, but most wood frames allow sufficient gap.

With windows recessed into a wall it may be possible to fit the glazing to enclose the whole window opening.

SEALED UNITS IN EXISTING FRAMES

Not all existing frames are suitable for sealed unit glazing, but for those that are, sealed unit double glazing is a neat and effective way of insulating.

The old frame must be capable of taking the weight of the two panes of glass. Measure up very carefully taking the width and height of the opening at several points and checking the diagonals. Give all these dimensions to your supplier and ask him to make an allowance for fitting the glass. Measure the depth of the window rebate on which the sealed unit will sit and take your supplier's advice on whether a straight-sided unit will fit or if you will need a stepped one.

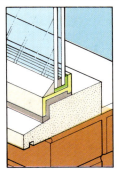
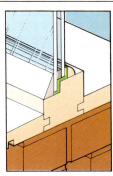

To ensure efficient insulation, the two panes of a sealed unit are mounted with an air-gap between. Where the window glazing rebate is wide enough, a straight sided unit may be fitted. If not, a stepped unit could be necessary. Not all frames are strong enough for fitting sealed unit double-glazing, due to the extra weight.

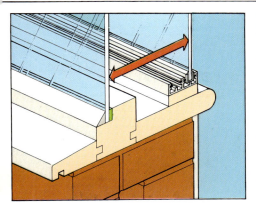

For sound as well as heat insulation a larger air-gap of at least 100mm is needed. Fit the glazing system to battens inside the window reveal.

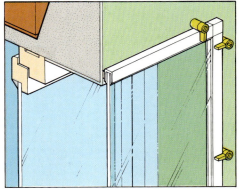

In some situations it may be possible to fit certain types of secondary double-glazing to the wall outside the window reveal, allowing a larger air-gap.

SEALED UNITS IN REPLACEMENT WINDOWS

Replacing your existing window frames with new ones just to get the heat-saving benefits of sealed unit double glazing would be very bad value but if you are thinking of replacement windows anyway – to replace old ones which are in poor condition – then it makes sense to have the new ones double glazed.

If you're going to have your new windows installed for you, shop around for the best price. Prices vary considerably and a firm may well be prepared to negotiate if they know there is competition. Remember that local builders can undertake this work and may well be cheaper than a specialist firm.

Most replacement windows are made-to-measure, but before you commit yourself to the expense of win-

Replacement windows are available in different materials ai·d styles.

Double-glazed patio doors in white PVC are virtually maintenance free.

dows specially made to fit your openings, find out from them whether there are standard size windows which will fit. Windows and patio doors in standard sizes are available off-the-shelf in wood, plastic and aluminium. You can also buy window kits in wood and aluminium which you use to build your own made-to-measure window.

Choosing the right material for the new frames is important. It will depend partly on whether you prefer the look of wood, aluminium or plastic, but there are practical considerations too and price to take into account.

Wooden windows are usually the cheapest. If the existing windows are wood, new wooden ones will usually be most in keeping with the house's architecture. By staining or painting you can have the frames any colour you want, but it means they require

regular maintenance, which you may well be hoping to avoid.

Aluminium window frames are slim and increase the area of the window which can let in light. The aluminium is virtually maintenance free, but most are set in a wooden subframe which does need regular attention.

Plastic window frames began to be installed widely in Britain only in the early 80's, and sceptics argue that the material is unproven in this country's climate.

However plastic windows have been successfully used on the continent, particularly in Germany, for years and it seems unlikely that things will be any different here. The plastic itself is virtually maintenance free and there is often no wooden subframe to worry about.

CURTAINS

Once drawn closed across a window, curtains can be as effective as double glazing. Make a point of drawing all the curtains in your house as soon as the sun goes down.

Lined curtains will retain most heat and the more material used to make the curtains the better. If they fall in generous folds, each fold will trap a pocket of air and improve the insulation. Special thermal linings can be used to improve the insulation still more. Don't fit curtains over radiators or stop them just short in such a way the heat will tend to rise behind the curtain. Either fit a shelf over the radiator or fit the curtains to hang on the window sill. If the curtain track stands out from the wall, stop air circulating down behind the curtains by fitting a pelmet.

A well-fitted pelmet stops cold air circulating from behind the curtains.

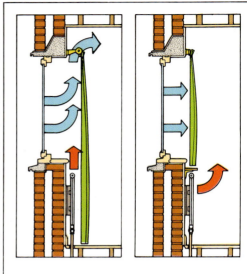

Never hang curtains in front of a radiator as it will trap the rising warm air. Either hang the curtains within the window reveal, or fit a radiator shelf.

Where there is no radiator below the window, curtains hanging to the floor are most efficient. If a radiator is fitted, either hang the curtains inside the window reveal or fit a radiator shelf to deflect the hot air.

Extra energy saving

When you've taken all the insulating measures in this book, you'll be able to turn down your heating controls and your bills for heating fuel will be much lower. But, to get the biggest savings, you need controls which will help you use your heating system economically. And, having insulated, it makes sense to cut out needless waste – a few commonsense measures will help here.

CUTTING OUT WASTE

- read your meters regularly to see how much electricity and gas you are using. Make a note of when you use it faster than normal and try to work out why

- turn the heating off at night – have it go off say half an hour before you normally go to bed; experiment to find the ideal length of time

- similarly, turn room heaters off ten minutes or so before you leave the room; the temperature will stay high for this short while and you'll save that much fuel

- don't leave outside doors open or open windows unnecessarily

- don't heat rooms you are not using – enough heat will escape into them from the rest of the house to keep the worst chill off

- have rooms in which you sit at a maximum temperature of 20°C. Hang a thermometer or digital temperature reader on the wall and turn the heating down when it gets too warm. Turning the heat down one degree from 21° to 20°C throughout the house can save 5% of your bills. Experiment with the lowest temperature you can stand, but don't let children or elderly people sit in rooms heated to less than 15°C

- don't run the central heating to supply less than four radiators; if you need to have only a few on, use room heaters instead

HOT WATER

- use hot water when it is available from the central heating, rather than at times when it will need a boost from an immersion heater

- save hot water by having showers instead of baths

Turning down the room thermostat, one degree, can save 5% on fuel bills.

- stop hot taps dripping at once

- if it takes a very long time for hot water to come through to a hot tap, in the kitchen perhaps, trace the pipes and insulate them. Consider fitting an instantaneous water heater

HEATING CONTROLS

You probably have a timer or programmer to switch your heating on and off two or more times a day. It should work in conjunction with a room thermostat to regulate the temperature. Thermostatic radiator valves, which can be fitted to replace the ordinary valve that is used to turn the radiator on and off, do the same job. They have the advantage that different rooms can be set to different temperatures.

The thermostat on your hot water cylinder should not be set above 60°C.

Thermostatic radiator valves allow each room's temperature to be set.

It's equally important to have a thermostat on your hot water cylinder to regulate the temperature of the stored hot water. Having a thermostat set to control the temperature to a maximum of 60°C not only saves money, but means that there is less chance of anyone scalding themselves. In hard water areas there's an added benefit that scale forms less quickly if the water is kept at temperatures below 60°.

A hot water cylinder thermostat is normally strapped to the cylinder and wired to open and shut a valve installed in the water heating pipework. It should also be wired to turn the boiler off when heat is not required for the radiators.

Advice and help

Use this checklist to decide how to spend your money on insulation. Starting with the jobs that cost only a few pounds and working up to those that cost several hundreds, even thousands, of pounds. And don't ignore the 'free' list, there are big savings to be made on your fuel bills from following even these simple tips.

INSULATION CHECKLIST

Free
- turn the heating controls down 1°C – you're unlikely to notice the difference
- keep doors to the outside closed as much as possible, invite doorstep callers in rather than standing with the door open
- turn the heating off in rooms that you don't regularly use
- wear extra clothing when the weather is colder
- tuck spare bedding round the hot water cylinder

Cost only a few pounds
- fitting a hot water cylinder jacket
- weatherstripping all external doors and internal doors to unheated rooms
- weatherstripping windows
- stopping other gaps which let heat escape to the outside – letterboxes etc
- fitting plastic film double glazing especially in rooms with north or east facing windows

Cost up to about £150
- installing loft insulation (don't forget to find out if you are eligible for a grant)
- fitting do-it-yourself double glazing in selected rooms – do windows in north and east facing rooms and rooms that you heat the most first
- fitting internal wall insulation in one room – do the room you heat most first
- installing ground floor insulation

Cost several hundreds of pounds
- installing cavity wall insulation
- fitting internal wall insulation throughout the house
- fitting DIY double glazing throughout the house

Cost several thousands of pounds
- professionally installed double glazing
- external wall insulation

The following organisations can give useful help and advice on various aspects of insulation.

British Board of Agrément
PO Box 195
Bucknalls Lane
Garston
Watford
Herts WD2 7NG

The Building Centre
in London at
26 Store Street
WC1E 7BT

and also in Birmingham, Bristol, Cambridge, Durham, Glasgow, Manchester, Nottingham and Southampton

Eurisol UK – Association of British Manufacturers of Mineral Insulating Fibres
St Paul's House
Edison Road
Bromley
Kent BR2 0EP

Glass & Glazing Federation
6 Mount Row
London W1Y 6DY

Heating and Ventilating Contractors Association
34 Palace Court
London WC2 4JG

National Cavity Insulation Association
PO Box 12
Haslemere
Surrey GU27 3AN

Your local British Gas and Electricity Board showrooms and Solid Fuel Advisory Service office will give advice on use of the relevant fuel.

Photography by Malcolm Pendrill.

All illustrations by Ron Haywood Art Group.

PRINTED IN BELGIUM BY

INTERNATIONAL BOOK PRODUCTION